When I Was a Child

Stories by Adell Wingo Carden

Arranged and Compiled by Vickie Carden Posey

Adell (on right) with younger brother, Buck, around 1930

Table of Contents

A Note on these Stories, Poems

Once, I think for my birthday, Mama recorded several cassette tapes of stories from her childhood. Often, especially when I researched family history, I had asked Mama about growing up in the south during the great depression. So Mama decided to just go ahead and put everything on tape. During this time, I'd call Mama on the phone, and Daddy would say that she was down in the basement recording. She spent hours on these tapes, and I am so grateful that she did. Afterwards, I listened to the tapes and thought how unique and interesting the words were. Just like poetry, I thought. Then I transcribed the tapes as accurately as I could, not wanting to lose the feel of Mama's language. Finally, I typed them into little stories and put a title on each one. Later, I began to think of the stories as little poems, so I simply arranged Mama's words into lines and stanzas to give them the shape of poetry. For this book, sometimes I've used a poetic device like repetition to emphasize something or simply shape the poem. In some cases, I've formed the words into a particular type of poem, like a syllabic (using the same number of syllables on each line). I shaped the story, "Snuff" into a pantoum, which made it the longest poem in the collection. All of the poems are set in and around, Bremen, my hometown, the place where Mama grew up and has lived all of her life. I've given the stories the structure of poetry, but the language is still Mama's.

Vickie Carden Posey, middle daughter

Working at Roland Brown's

Daddy worked in the fields
and got paid by the hour,
and Mama and Daddy took care of the cows.
Mama got up early in the morning,
crossed the branch,
and went down to the Brown's house.
They had two cows.

Mama and Daddy both did the feeding,
but Mama did the milking - morning and night.
I don't know if they gave Mama the milk
or if we had to pay for it, but we got some.
Mr. Brown grew turnip greens, potatoes, corn,
and cotton that he took to the gin.
Children's work was picking bugs
off Irish potato plants.

Brush Broom

There was no grass in our yard, just hard dirt,
so we swept it.
We used a brush broom made of honeysuckle.
We'd throw things out in the yard,
and when there was too much trash,
we burned it.

In the fall, we looked for broom straw
and brought it home
in big bundles about four foot high.
We'd take a cord and tie it around the straw midways –
tight, and make a broom.

Then we'd pull the little limbs off it.
This was called cleaning it.
We'd wrap the string from the middle,
all the way to the top - real tight.
We never bought a broom.

We made several at a time
so we'd have one when one wore out.
Mops were shuck mops made with a piece of wood,
about one inch thick and four inches wide.
We'd bore holes and stick shucks in the holes.

The end of a shuck was hard
so you could stick it in.
We scrubbed floors with the shuck mop and lye or sand.
Our wood floors had cracks,
so the water just drained right through.

We didn't do it during the winter;
it was too cold. We used Red Devil lye.

Yankee Dime

Uncle Homer and Aunt Ester Lena,
they went to live on the county road.
Ester Lena would plow just like a man,
so she raised the crop, and he hired out.

We'd walk to Grandpa's and Uncle Homer's on weekends,
and Ester Lena always made us a big pudding—
in a dishpan. They had cows and always had milk,
even if they didn't have much else.

She cooked that pudding—pineapple or
banana—on the wood stove, and when the fire got started,
you couldn't turn it down. It would scorch
unless you kept on stirring.

I was the oldest grandchild,
so she called on me to help. Don't know
why her own daughter, cousin Vivian, couldn't do it.
But I liked Aunt Ester Lena and did what she said.

I was small but wanted to be just like my aunt,
fat and happy, so I ate as much as I could.
She told me if I'd stir that pudding,
she'd dance at my wedding, and I thought to myself

"That would be a sight to see!" Or she
said she'd give me a yankee dime.
I didn't know what that was, but it sounded good,
so I stirred and stirred.

She never danced at my wedding, but
she always hugged my neck and kissed my cheek.
If I had all the dimes she promised,
I'd be rich.

Sit to Bedtime

After work in the fields, we would visit around.
Grown-ups talked while kids played.
Everyone stayed until it got to be bedtime.
We called this, "sit to bedtime."
Ollie and Lois lived on one side of the Railroad track,
and we lived on the other,
and they started having chili suppers.
This was the first time I knew about chili powder and chili,
and boy was it good.

Boy was it good.
We ate it with soup crackers, and if they didn't make chili,
they made oyster stew, but I didn't like that.
Sometimes the chili didn't have much beef,
but it always had pintos and pork and beans.
If we didn't have meat,
we just made it without.
We always liked to eat it hot
and made it hotter every time.

Milking

When I learned to milk,
I'd take water to
wash the teats off. I
had to milk by hand.

Sometimes it was cold,
but the milk would be
hot, and I couldn't
stand the smell. I don't

drink milk till today
because of this. I'd
bring in the milk, strain
it in a flour

sack, and then cover
it. We covered most
things with flour sacks
or sheeting because

there were no lids. We
tied a string around
it to keep out the
flies. We milked night and

day and set the milk
by the fireplace in
the winter time. The
little ones would churn.

If milk got too hot,
it turned to puffy
butter. I liked it.

Snow and Soot

There was a big snow right after we moved to the place on Highway 27,
just before Christmas. We needed wood, so Daddy cut up a log.
We couldn't hardly stay warm, it was so cold that year.
The snow came earlier than we had thought it would.
The roads were slicky, and there was a truck coming along the curve
loaded with starch. It run off the road, it was so slippery.

Daddy said he woke up in the morning and had to knock snow off his face.
The house was not sealed and the snow came right in.
It was rough in the beginning, but we made a crop that year
and had lots of pecan trees. It was the year Dee started to school.
She didn't ride the school bus. Maybe we weren't on the bus route.
There were just a few buses back then.

Deloris crawled under the house
and cut her toe
and couldn't finish school that year.
We put soot on it.

Marbles in the Water Trough

We lived at the Biggers' place,
when Grandma Mauk lived in Tallapoosa.
Mr. Biggers lived on the other side of Buchanan where we sharecropped.
We worked the land and divided the main crop with the owner.

We divided the main crop with the owner
when me and Buck were about 12 and 10, and Daddy farmed on halves.
If we got our own cotton planted and picked,
we hired out and picked cotton for other people.

We picked cotton for other people, but
I couldn't pick much more than 100 pounds a day and earned about 75 cents.
In the fall, we got caught up and picked for Mr. Biggers, and
we were supposed to get paid.

We were supposed to get paid,
and then we were going to Tallapoosa to see Grandma Mauk.
But when we went to get our money, he wouldn't pay us.
We passed a barn with a water trough to feed cattle, and we thought of an idea.

We thought of an idea.
There was a pipe that ran from the trough to the well,
so me and Buck decided to drop marbles in the trough to stop up the water.
We always played marbles and always had some in our pockets.

We always had some in our pockets,
so as we walked toward home, after not being paid,
we dropped marbles in the water.
We were so aggravated that he didn't pay us.

He didn't pay us
when we'd worked so hard and wanted to go see Grandma.

Valentines

I never remember having any books in the house.
Later on, we got an almanac and the Sears Roebuck catalog.
Mama liked to read "True Story" books,
and she'd get one from a neighbor every once in a while.
I don't ever remember reading one though.

She'd also get postcards and write off for samples.
That was probably the only cologne or powder she ever got back then.
She also wrote in and got a whole sample wallpaper book.
It was a pretty good size book, and she used it to make us valentines to take to school.
We didn't have any store bought valentines.

Snuff

When I was a little girl,
My grandmother used to dip snuff.
It came in a little round tin box.
She carried it around in her apron pocket.

My grandmother used to dip snuff.
I always stayed with her a lot.
She carried it around in her apron pocket.
Me and Grandma went out picking blackberries.

I always stayed with her a lot.
She wanted me to sit down and not get in the briars.
Me and Grandma went out picking blackberries.
"Sit here," she said, "while I pick the berries."

She wanted me to sit down and not get in the briars.
"I'll let you hold my snuff box."
"Sit here," she said, "while I pick the berries."
We didn't have boxes and things to play with.

"I'll let you hold my snuff box."
The snuff box was real cute.
We didn't have boxes and things to play with.
I remember her picking and me holding the box.

The snuff box was real cute.
I handed her the snuff box back.
I remember her picking and me holding the box.
"I don't want to hold your snuff box no more," I said.

I handed her the snuff box back.
I'd eaten about half the snuff.
"I don't want to hold your snuff box no more," I said.
It really made me sick.

I'd eaten about half the snuff.
It came in a little round tin box.
It really made me sick
when I was a little girl.

The Circle Tailed Skirt

Grandma Mauk had come and brought me
a circle-tailed skirt. She showed me
how to cut it out. I can still
cut that skirt out. Took two paper
sacks, put them together, and cut

out the pattern. We all had to
make our own patterns back then. The
bonnet patterns and some other
things were handed down. We had no
newspapers, so we used paper

sacks. This skirt was red-checked gingham
and I was tiny. Thought I was
cute, thought I was something
with my circle-tailed skirt and permanent.

Post Toasties

Mama said when she went to work
and got a paycheck
that she wanted herself a bait of cornflakes
and buttered toast.
She loved buttered toast till the day she died.

We had a man
who brought ice for the ice box,
and we would
put a piece of ice in the milk
to cool it down.

Every Friday night
when Mama come home, she'd bring
a big box of Post Toasties,
and that's what we'd have for supper,
with sweet milk, ice cold.

The Purchase

I had made about a dollar
        and we were going to town--
        to Tallapoosa—in a wagon.
We went to a store called Mitnicks,
        owned by a Jewish family.
It was a general store that had
        material, clothes, overalls, and such.

I went to the store
        and bought me some socks
        and enough material to make a dress.
Grandma Mauk was a good seamstress,
        and she could help me.
When I got through with my purchase,
        I had a dime left,
        so I bought me a little pocketbook.
I bought all this stuff from working on the farm.

Sweet Gum

I walked to school with Mildred and Rayford,
Grandma Mauk's two youngest.
I was in third grade when we moved to Roland Brown's place.
Mildred was four years older than me,
but we'd walk all over the farm—about a hundred acres--
to hunt sweet gum trees.

We'd get the resin from the tree,
and that was our chewing gum.
It would stick to your teeth at first,
but after a while,
it got better.

Apples

Roland Brown's place had lots of apple trees,
and we enjoyed them, especially me.
I always loved apples.
We ate fresh apples and dried apples.
Once, somebody gave Daddy a whole bushel
of apples that he was going to save for Christmas.

He was going to save them for Christmas,
and put them under the bed where I slept,
thinking they would be safe.
But I could reach the basket, and
every morning, I slipped my hand
under the bed and got an apple.

I got an apple,
and I'd get under the cover and eat it
until I ate about a peck of apples
before Christmas.
When Daddy got the basket out,
he wondered where all those apples went to.

Popcorn

I've always been real crazy about
popcorn.
Once I went to spend the night with a neighbor, and they had a whole room of
popcorn,
so when I got ready to go home, I just took me an ear of
popcorn
home. Mama asked me about it, and I said that I just got me one ear,
but Mama made me take that
popcorn
back to the house and tell them I stole some
popcorn.
That's one thing—you didn't take anything that didn't belong to you, not even one ear of
popcorn.

BB Gun

Uncle Willie was working in Atlanta and bought Buck and Willie a BB gun.
We all played with guns.
Daddy and the boys had guns hanging over the door.
All people had shot guns, not pistols, but shot guns to kill rabbits and squirrels.
Most every house had a gun.

We had a barn with a loft,
and next door was a lady
who would come to our house to draw water.
She was the one who lived closest to the Railroad tracks.
This lady really liked Bill, and gave him a nickel or a penny.

Me and Buck got mad since she didn't give us any money,
so we got in the loft
and shot at her when she went to the outside toilet.
We didn't like her.

Two for One

When I was 10 years old, my job
was to drop guano in the field.
We'd put a peck sack around us
and drop handfuls every step
and someone would come along behind
and drop the corn. Everyone
cleared out stables and barns
to use as fertilizer.

About this time, me and Buck
began to work in the fields a lot more.
We'd work for 75 cents a day.
The two of us would be on the same row,
hoeing and chopping, and would equal one adult.
When we were old enough,
we'd pick cotton each fall
instead of going to school.

Bitterweed

We had buttermilk to make bread
and would divide with the neighbors.
I didn't like sweet milk much,
but I could eat buttermilk and onions pretty good.

If a cow ate bitterweed, you couldn't use the milk.
Most people pulled up all the bitterweed
and wild onions because it would taste in the milk.
Milk would be so bitter that we fed it to the pigs.

We might use it in bread,
but you couldn't drink it.

Choke it, Zootie!

When we lived at Roland Brown's place,
we had neighbors by the name of McElroy.
The mother's name was Zootie,
and they were the only folks around who had a car.

They were so stingy. Mrs. McElroy would take the beans
and boil them with lots of soup
and they'd eat bean soup and corn bread.
She stretched everything.

That car wouldn't pull up a hill,
so they would turn around and back it up.
They'd get so far, and all us kids
would get out in the back yard and say,

"here comes the car!"
We would watch them come up the hill,
and some man always yelled,
"Choke it, Zootie!!"

Eating at Grandma's

Eating at Grandma Mauk's and Grandma Wingo's were different things.
At Grandma Mauk's, you could go in and eat anything in her kitchen any time.
But at Grandma Wingo's, we were never allowed to go into her kitchen and eat.
Grandpa Wingo always had a lot of meat, especially pork from hogs,
and Grandma Wingo would fry a big plate of ham.

I can see it now on a brown platter, stored under a warming cloth,
bread wrapped up in another cloth to keep it from getting cold and hard.
She served it with red-eye gravy.
Sometimes we had streak-o-lean.
There was always ham left, but we couldn't go in and get it.

Grandma wouldn't let us.
At her house, you either ate at meal time or you didn't eat.
You didn't go in and get anything after meals,
and we knew not to ask.
I can't remember ever trying to slip into her kitchen.

Baby Willie and the Cotton

At Felton, we were picking cotton to make a living,
and we had bundles of cotton on the porch.
Daddy was always playing with us,
so one day, he buried me and Buck in the cotton.

We thought it was lots of fun,
so when Mama and Daddy went back to the field
and left me and Buck to watch baby Willie,
we decided we'd bury him in the cotton.

We didn't know we weren't supposed
to cover him all the way up, and so we did.
Then Daddy hollered and
asked us how Willie was doing.

We yelled, "We buried him in the cotton,"
and they come back in a hurry.

FDR and the WPA

Grandma Mauk moved from Roland Brown's place
to Tallapoosa and lived out in "old town."
Ray, Emily, and Mildred were still living at home.
The others were married.
During that time, FDR put people to work on the WPA,
cleaning roadways and other things.
Grandma went to work with one of these programs
doing sewing for widow women,
and she had a little better income.

From then on, she lived in town until she moved to Atlanta.
Emily went to Atlanta to work,
and later on, Grandma bought a boarding house there.
We went over to see her in an A-model.
We'd get all dressed up to go to Grandma's.
Went to East Point, I think.
You'd have thought we were going to be gone for a month,
the way we were packing up and getting ready to go.

Guitar

When Mama went to work at Sewell's,
I quit school to keep Darrell,
And I also had to watch the other children.
I was in charge because I was the oldest,
and Daddy told the boys to help me.
He told Buck to bring in the wood
so that I could cook bread,
but lots of time, he wouldn't,
so I had to chase him all over. We'd scuffle.
When we got up older, he was better about bringing in the wood.

He was better about bringing in the wood,
but one day, there was another issue
because somebody give Buck and Bill a guitar.
They got up a fight about the guitar
and went in the bedroom
and pulled the bed against the door,
so I couldn't get in.
They were pretty big boys at that time
and were fighting about that guitar.

They were fighting about that guitar.
I was about fifteen, so Buck was thirteen and Bill was eleven.
When I finally got in there,
they were still going at it,
but I saw the guitar laying on the bed,
so I got it and rammed them over the head with it
to get them separated.
I had to do it;
I was afraid they'd keep fighting
and hurt one another.

Potato Chips

We didn't get to go to Grandma's boarding house that much—
about twice a year—because she lived so far away, maybe 50 miles, in Atlanta.
We went by the Gordon's potato chip factory on the way there,
and we would always get a peck-sack full of potato chips on the way back.

They would fill up our brown paper sack with potato chips,
and all us kids would eat them on the way home.
At the time, Mama worked at Sewell's, Darrell was a baby, and I was about 15.
We enjoyed those potato chips.

Sewing

My Grandmas were real sweet, and I liked
to go see them both. Grandma Mauk sewed
dresses and things, but Grandma Wingo
pieced quilts. Grandma Mauk was a very
good seamstress, and she always wanted
us to cut out something and sew it.
I made dresses when I was still little.

She always wanted us girls to piece
quilts and sew. We had boxes of scraps
from all kinds of things, and we used these
to make quilts. I never did learn to
embroider or crochet much, but
Grandma Mauk was good at all of it.
She made all of Mildred's dresses and

people talked about how well-dressed
she always was.

Being a Lady

Grandma Wingo was strict about children.
She thought they should be seen and not heard.
You'd think Grandma Mauk would have been stricter,
but it was the other way around.

Grandma Wingo hounded us girls about manners.
She had all boys, but told us girls,
"A lady does not sit with her legs crossed.
Her feet should be on the floor."

She said, "a whistling girl and a crowing hen,
never come to no good end."
That was Grandma's way of keeping me and Vivian straight,
her granddaughters, since she had only boys.

The Haircut

Daddy always cut our hair.
He had clippers, and he'd just sit down and start cutting.
We always had to wear our hair short because long hair was hard to keep clean.
So when our hair grew out, he'd cut it.

He always bobbed mine right below the ears.
When I was 14 or 15, I didn't want my hair cut this way anymore,
but he cut it anyway, and I cried and cried.
I said, "I'm going to go get me a permanent,

and I'm going to have it charged to you,
and if you kill me, you'll just kill me."
I just had a big fit. So me and Mama
got our first permanents for $1.50 each.

It looked like they were electrocuting us.
Our hair was rolled
and they hooked us up to the heat.
I was real proud of that perm.

Rank Meat

Once Mrs. Biggers wanted me to come
and
help her clean up her smokehouse. I went,
and
we found a piece of meat in the meat box that was so rank it had turned yellow—
not a very big piece--
but
she was so excited that we found meat underneath the salt. She took it out
and
washed it
and
sliced it
and
cooked some green beans with that rank meat.
Those were the best green beans.
Now I wouldn't eat beans cooked like that,
but
they were so good.

Baching

We left Felton because Daddy didn't like the house.
We had a fireplace there, but the house wasn't sealed.
So Daddy went back to the sawmill, even though Mama had it real bad.
She had to stay home with all of us kids with no telephone
or any way to get in touch with anybody.

At that time, Daddy would go baching.
He would leave on Monday morning and go stay at the sawmill,
and he'd come home on the weekends.
Once he was coming home, and we had real big rains.
The river went over the bridges and got out into the bottoms.

He walked through holding onto the rail of the bridge,
with a box of groceries on one shoulder
and a sack of flour on another,
trying to get home so we'd have something to eat.
We never had much, but he brought us peanut butter.

Spelling Bee

In the 1940's, there were two houses on the farm, and Daddy had rented the whole farm.
We lived in the big house, and he rented out the little one.
It was a nice house--2 rooms and a shed room.
It rented for about $3 a month.
A little girl lived with her parents in the rented house, and she could spell anything.
We were in the same grade.

She won a spelling bee.
I could never spell, and I didn't like her much because she was too smart.
She got to go to school; her mama let her go to school all the time.
Me and Buck didn't get that much school.
It was hard to get even as much as we did.
We were always having to catch up with things.

A Piece of Chicken

When Grandma Mauk moved to Atlanta,
she learned city ways.
She was raised in the country, but found her way around.
She could take you all over downtown Atlanta – anywhere you wanted to go.
We'd ride the trolleys to Rich's and Davison's.

She ran a boarding house close to Georgia Tech and the Fox theatre
and made Sunday lunch with rice, fried chicken, and English peas.
One day, Emily fixed dinner and
saved all the chicken backs for Grandma.
When Grandma come in, Em said,

"I saved you your favorite piece of chicken,
the one you always eat." Then Grandma told her,
"All the time you kids were growing up,
I had to eat chicken backs
so ya'll could have a good piece of chicken.

That's what moms do, you know.
Now that you've all grown up and I can afford it,
I'll have me a good piece of chicken.
I don't really like chicken backs.
Not much meat on them."

Bleach

When Grandma Mauk
was at our house,
she'd say,
"don't use that bleach--
it'll eat your clothes up."
But bleach made clothes white,
so we used it.

Then Grandma would beat her clothes
with a battling stick.
I thought to myself
that nothing was harder on clothes
than that.

Whiskey

When Uncle Willie worked off somewhere, probably Atlanta,
he came home to stay with Grandpa and they found a still.
In my younger days, I remember Daddy drinking some.
He'd get drunk at times and come home and be smelling like whiskey.
I always knew when he'd been drinking.

Once, Daddy put all his whiskey in little bottles.
I don't know where the bottles came from,
but it made me so mad for him to be drinking in front of the little kids.
So I got Mama's snuff boxes and filled every one of the bottles with snuff.
I figured when he found this, he'd know I done it, and he'd give me a whipping.

But he never said anything about it, never mentioned it.
And he never drank that much anymore.
We always kept whiskey for cough syrup.
During election time, politicians would buy us whiskey
or give us a dollar to vote for them.

People would take the dollar or whiskey,
but then vote for who they wanted.
Daddy always went to the court house and voted. I don't think Mama went.
But politicians were always passing out whiskey
and money to get you to vote for them.

Frog Gigging

Growing up, I played with lots of boy cousins
that were around my age. Rayford, my uncle,
was only nine months older than I was. I
was a big tomboy. One day I was going
walking when we lived on the Manghum place.

There was an underpass where water ran like
a little branch, and highway 78
went over it. A bunch of us were walking
and saw a frog, and we all started throwing
rocks at it. I said that I could hit it, and I did.

Back then, people ate frogs or frog legs. People went
frog gigging. You would get a long pole with a
point on the end. You'd shine a lantern or some
light at the frog and then stick it with the sharp point.
So I killed the frog - instead of one of the boys,

and we brought it home for Mama to fry,
but I cried because I killed it. I have
not eaten frog since then. I really didn't
think I could hit the frog, but I did.
I guess I was just showing off.

Lard bucket

When Daddy worked for the sawmill,
he carried lunch in a lard bucket, a gallon one.

Mama would get up and make biscuits,
and he'd take seven or eight of them for lunch.

He got 75 cents to $1.00 a day for work at that time,
but nobody made much money then.

Peaches

Around 1939 or 40, we moved to Bremen
on Cash Town Road below the red house
and stayed about two years.
We were right near the railroad track,
but there was one house even closer.
Daddy worked on the Manghum farm in the peach orchards.

They grew cotton too.
We farmed the land up on the hill
and had a corn patch behind.
Sam House's daddy used to walk
through our yard to go to work at the school.
He was janitor there and fired the boiler.

Daddy and Mama and all of us did crops,
but when the peaches came in,
we'd all pick peaches,
and Mr. Manghum would ship them all over.
There were four or five houses of people
who worked in the peach orchard and tended the land.

Skunk

We moved to Felton, Georgia
and Daddy helped a man farm.
This is where I started to
School—at Felton when I was
around 5 or 6 years old.

I remember Mama then,
taking me up the road to
go to school and then walking
with someone, but I don't know
who. We all had to walk back

then since there were no buses.
When we lived in Felton, a
skunk got in our house and
we couldn't get it out, so
my Daddy shot it, and it

sprayed the whole house. We had to
leave the house for a long time.
We had to bury Daddy's
overalls because they smelled
so bad – even though Daddy

didn't have too many clothes.

Playing

We played outside with cans and boxes,
and we'd pretend to churn and make it foam.

We'd play house by putting rocks around the part we called our house.
We made toys out of May pops.

Grandma Wingo loved to eat May pops.
We'd stick broom straws into May pops and make all kinds of animals.

We'd take leaves and pin them together to make hats and headbands.
Most of our toys were homemade.

We would play with anything that would roll.
We had heard of telephones but didn't have one,

so we took cans and put cords between them and pretended.

Making baskets

Grandpa was good at making cotton baskets.
He used white oak strips.
He would break a piece of glass
and scrape the strips to make them slick,
to get rid of the roughness.

Certain types of wood and the season,
when sap was rising, affected the strips.
I don't think Daddy ever made baskets.
We picked cotton in baskets till there was enough for a bale.
Grandpa sat under the shed and scraped till the fuzz was off.

Tea

When Grandma Mauk moved to Tallapoosa,
she would fix Sunday dinner.
She was always a good cook.
One day she said, "We're having tea."

None of us knew what tea was.
Most of the time, children drank milk--
buttermilk, sweet milk--or water.
When Grandma poured us ice tea,

we thought it was the horriblest tasting stuff
we'd ever had in our lives.
Now I like tea, but it took me a long time.
At first, tea reminded me of liver powder.

Sleeping arrangements

We didn't have enough beds
so all us children had to sleep in the same one,
four of us crossways.
If company came,
then the kids slept on pallets.

When I was older,
I slept by myself in the bed we saved for company.
The others were jealous.
But I was the oldest and could be counted on
not to wet the bed.

In the back room,
away from the fire place,
we had to have a bunch of quilts
to keep us warm.

The Gash

When we lived at Mr. Manghum's place in Bremen,
I jumped off the porch
and hit some broken glass from a fruit jar
somebody had thrown out.

Blood just shot out of my ankle,
and we couldn't get it stopped.
Someone ran in and got some soot from the chimney
and slathered it on the cut.

It made the blood clot.
Cuts were doctored with kerosene.
The gash was about one inch long.
It stayed black for years.

Cedar Tree

One year I was out in the pasture
and found a pretty little cedar tree.
I was ten or twelve years old,
and I brought it back,
dug a hole,
set it out,
and watered it.

Then Grandma and Grandpa came and said,
"Who put the cedar tree out there?"
I told them I had,
and Grandma Wingo went out,
pulled my cedar tree up,
and took it out of the yard.

She said, "You can't set a cedar tree out.
When that tree gets big enough
to shade your grave,
you'll die."

Glossary

General definitions of terms were taken from Random House Webster's College Dictionary. I've included the definition that most closely fits the meaning in the poem and the part of speech that is represented in the poem.

Terms

1. A-model (noun) – An early type of automobile produced by the Ford Company. The A-model, which first came out in 1927, was the second big success for Ford, after the Model T. Production of the A-model ended in 1932, after almost 5 million had been produced.
2. Bale (noun) - a large bundle, especially one tightly compressed and secured by wires, cords, or the like.
3. Bait (noun) - The closest definition to the meaning in this poem is labeled archaic: to stop for food or refreshment during a journey. In the poem, "bait" refers to eating your fill, eating as much as you want.
4. Bitterweed (noun) – The dictionary did not list this particular word, but online sources define it as: any of various plants containing a bitter principle, as those of the genus Picris. In the poem, bitterweed is a plant/weed that grows wild in pastures and smells like onions.
5. Bottoms (noun) – low alluvial land next to a river. Sometimes called bottom land, it is good for crops but easily flooded.
6. Branch (noun) – a tributary stream or any stream that is not a large river or a bayou.
7. Choke (verb) – to enrich the fuel mixture of an internal combustion engine by diminishing the air supply to the carburetor. In the poem, choking the car refers to a method of starting a car when you're having trouble cranking it. With some early motors, there was a button to push and "choke" the motor.
8. Churn (verb) – to agitate in order to make into butter. As a noun, it means: a container or machine in which cream or milk is agitated to make butter.
9. Draw (verb) – to bring, take, or pull out, as from a receptacle or source: *To draw water from a well.*
10. Fired the boiler (verb) – Fired: to supply with fuel; attend to the fire. Boiler: a closed vessel in which water is heated to make steam for powering, turbines, supplying heat, etc.
11. Frog gigging (verb) – to catch fish or frogs with a gig (shortened from fishgig, a kind of harpoon)

12. Guano (noun) – 1. a natural manure composed chiefly of the excrement of sea birds, found especially on islands near the Peruvian coast. 2. Any similar substance, as an artificial fertilizer made from fish. Southerners sometimes pronounce the word with an "R" at the end – "guaner."
13. Irish potato (noun) – an Irish potato is simply a regular white potato as opposed to a sweet potato. As a root vegetable it must be dug out of the ground. It became known as "Irish," perhaps because of the well-known potato famine in Ireland.
14. Lye (noun) – a highly concentrated, aqueous solution of potassium hydroxide or sodium hydroxide.
15. Material (noun) – a textile fabric
16. Maypop (noun) – the edible fruit of a passion flower.
17. Peck (noun) – a dry measure of 8 quarts; a fourth of a bushel.
18. Permanent (noun) – shortened from "permanent wave." A wave or curl set into the hair by the application of chemical preparations and/or heat and lasting for a number of months.
19. Post Toasties (noun) – this is the brand name of perhaps the first version of cornflakes. It was toasted corn (in flake form) produced by the Post company, hence Post Toasties.
20. Rank (adjective) – having an offensive smell or taste
21. Red Devil lye (noun) – this is the brand name of lye that was commonly used in cleaning during the 1930s.
22. Red-eye gravy (noun) – This term was not in the dictionary, but some information was online. Red-eye gravy, sometimes called poor man's gravy, is particularly southern and uses the drippings of pan-fried pork mixed with black coffee and sometimes other ingredients such as butter and broth to produce a thin sauce. Red eye gravy is different from other gravies that are thickened with flour. Another southern favorite, sawmill gravy, calls for the same drippings as red-eye gravy (usually sausage, bacon, or country ham) but also flour and then milk or water mixed in to produce a very thick sauce.
23. Sharecropped (verb) – the practice of a tenant farmer paying as rent a share of his crop, farming someone else's land and giving them a portion of the crops as payment. Sharecropping was a standard way of living for many southerners who did not own land themselves. The tenant family benefitted from having a place to live (on the farm), growing food for themselves, and selling crops (after they had given the owners their "share."). "Farming on halves," meant that the tenant farmer gave half of his crop to the owner. Woody Guthrie refers to sharecropping in his song, "I Ain't Got No Home" when he says, "I was farmin on the share and always I was poor/My crops I laid into the banker's store."
24. Sheeting (noun) – a broad, relatively thin surface, layer, or covering. In the poem, it is fabric (probably inexpensive cotton), like sheets used on beds.

25. Shuck (noun) – 1. A husk or pod, as the outer covering of corn, hickory nuts, etc. 2. Something useless or worthless. In the poems, the shucks are from corn and were certainly not worthless. They were put to good use.
26. Smokehouse (noun) – a building or place in which meat, fish, etc are cured with smoke.
27. Snuff (noun) – a preparation of tobacco, either powdered and taken into the nostrils by inhalation or ground and placed between the cheek and gum. During the time of these poems, lots of people dipped snuff, including my grandmother and some great grandmothers. At the time, it seemed like the men took their tobacco by smoking or chewing, but the women took theirs by dipping. Dipping meant that the person took a small amount of snuff, put it in their mouths (usually just inside the lower lip), and held it there, occasionally spitting. I've heard that at the Buchanan courthouse there used to be a spittoon for folks who dipped or chewed. Another word for spittoon, cuspidor, is defined as: a large bowl, often of metal, serving as a receptacle for spit, especially from chewing tobacco.
28. Soot (noun) – a black carbonaceous substance produced during incomplete combustion of coal, wood, oil, etc, rising in fine particles that adhere to and blacken surfaces on contact. Evidently, during the time of these stories, soot was thought to have healing properties.
29. Starch (noun) – a commercial preparation of this substance (the white tasteless, solid carbohydrate, occurring in some plants) used to stiffen textile fabrics in laundering.
30. Streak-o-lean (noun) – This term was not in the dictionary, but parts of it were. Streak: a long, narrow mark, smear, band of color, or the like, a vein; stratum: streaks of fat in meat. Lean: (or meat) containing little or no fat. So Streak-o-lean means there's a streak of lean meat in what is otherwise all fat. Fat back, another type of southern pork, is all fat and is cut and cooked much like bacon.
31. Sweet gum (noun) – a tall, aromatic tree of the witch hazel family, native to the eastern U.S. with star-shaped leaves and fruits in rounded, bur-like clusters. Also called red gum.
32. Trough (noun) – pronounced "trof." A long, narrow, open receptacle, usually boxlike in shape, used chiefly to hold water or food for animals.
33. Yankee dime (noun) – This term is not in the standard dictionary but can be found online. It is a quick, innocent kiss, usually on the cheek of a child. I'm not sure of the origin. In the south, the term "Yankee" can be suspect, but the term "dime" refers to something of value.

Places

1. Bremen – the setting for these poems is in and around Bremen, a small town in Northwest Georgia that used to be a thriving factory town. During the time of the poems, the factories were just getting started, but soon there would be so many factories producing clothing that Bremen called itself "The Clothing Center of the South." Early on, Bremen was known as Kramer, after a German immigrant who had settled there. But Kramer wanted to honor his home country by naming the town Bremen, after the city in Germany. Although the names are spelled the same, they are pronounced differently, the Georgia version having a long "e" in the first syllable.
2. Tallapoosa – a small town west of Bremen and very close to the border with Alabama. Tallapoosa was a thriving city during the time of these poems and used to have a resort-like hotel. Tallapoosa is an Indian name, but the city was actually named after the Tallapoosa River. An earlier name for the city was "Possum Snout," and today the city holds an annual Possum drop every New Year's Eve.
3. Buchanan – the county seat of Haralson County. The oldest incorporated city in the county, Buchanan was named for James Buchanan, the 15th president of the United States, who served only one term, 1857-1861, just before the Civil War. Buchanan was the only bachelor to serve as president and was sometimes called a "doughface," a Northerner who sympathized with the South. He was succeeded by Abraham Lincoln. Buchanan High School was always Bremen's fiercest rival.
4. Felton – a small, unincorporated community in northwest Georgia, between Buchanan and Cedartown.
5. East Point – A suburb of Atlanta (southwest). The Hartsfield Jackson International Airport that serves Atlanta was built close to this area.

Acknowledgements

Thanks to everyone who contributed to this book – to those who read the manuscript and offered feedback or helped with photos and other parts: my husband, Derrell Posey; my sisters, Barbara Stegall and Patsy Bilbo; my daughter and her husband, Lee and Carl Pike. Thanks to my son, John, and his wife, Sally, along with their children: Luke, Ethan, Grace, Jude, and Silas - for continuing to show us all of the wonders of childhood. Thanks to the Warren P. Sewell Memorial Library in Bremen, Georgia, for hosting a book signing for this work. When I lived in Bremen, the only library was at the school and not available in the long, hot Georgia summers. I am happy that Bremen now has its own beautiful library – one that I visit whenever I'm back in town. I am especially grateful to Lisa Walton-Cagle, Branch Manager of the library; and Pat Johnson, Program Coordinator; for their support in sharing this work. Thanks to my father, Johnnie Carden, who passed away in 2014. He loved books, especially the Bible, and was a writer too – producing hundreds of sermons and other works during his lifetime. Finally, a huge debt of gratitude to Adell Agnes Wingo Carden, my mother and a great storyteller, who shares her life stories with an authentic voice and a genuine love for the people and places she talks about. She is an inspiration for others to share their own stories.

Vickie Carden Posey

Copies of this book can be ordered through Lulu (www.lulu.com)

and Amazon (www.amazon.com)

www.ingramcontent.com/pod-product-compliance
Ingram Content Group UK Ltd.
Pitfield, Milton Keynes, MK11 3LW, UK
UKHW041839200726
13854UKWH00003BA/1211

9 781365 493195